MEANWHILE

Cynthia Rodríguez

Burning Eye

This edition published by Burning Eye Books 2020

www.burningeye.co.uk

@burningeyebooks

Burning Eye Books
15 West Hill, Portishead, BS20 6LG

ISBN 978-1-911570-94-3

MEANWHILE

Cynthia Rodríguez (Monterrey, 1986) is a Mexican-British writer and performer based in Leicester. International, intersectional and interdisciplinary, Rodríguez uses poetry to convey everyday realities that may remain untold in media, particularly on feminist issues, cultural and countercultural shock, rites of passage and self-preservation. Mouthy Poets alumna and DIY punk artist at heart, her work has been featured in several zines and independent anthologies, including *Welcome to Leicester* (eds Emma Lee and Ambrose Musiyiwa), the *Black Flamingo Zine* (eds Dean Atta and Ben Connors) and *Do Something* (ed. Selina Lock). On stage, Rodríguez has opened for renowned artists such as Lydia Towsey, Hannah Swings, Caroline Bird, Lauren John Joseph and Jamie Thrasivoulou.

*If you find yourself reflected in these pages,
it is because they are for you.*

CONTENTS

LIMINAL INHABITANT

In the gaps between your furniture I live,
the flickering in your telly as you switch,
the murmurs grey between your radio stations,
the glue that sticks together your books and magazines.

I live in millimetric awkward silences,
crossfading songs in your recommended playlist.
The pressure on a can when you crack it open,
thumbs on caps lift from the bottle before the fizz.

I am in the impulse, not the run.
The deep breath before the scream.
Once the joke makes sense, not the laughter.
The wet eyes leading to the tears.

I am captured in the moment
before the pen meets the paper.
The interstice, the intersection.
Lines that circle on a diagram.

Airports, bus stops, tram stations and docks,
the nerves at ceremonies about to start.

I am in your garage, in your porch,
about to leave, about to come,
inhabiting liminality.

I take this lengua mi
a perro que
mother tongue
a goat, chasing the sun.

y digo que no soy de aqui
where's that accent from

Mexico? Ah Michoacán
e for a drag
mber. luna va
can't remember
mbar
estu

THE OUTSTANDING MIGRANT

NATURALISATION

We have finally proved to them
we belong in a place
where as soon as they are born – I suppose –
the midwife demands they belt
in the right order
the names of the wives of Henry VIII.
That's why babies cry.

They shout,
Excuse me,
but I barely know my parents
and siblings, in case I have them.
All I want right now
is to go back into the swimming pool of goo
and close my eyes –
is that what you call them? Eyes? –
because the light on the ceiling is unbearable.

Have I reincarnated in the wrong place and time
and skin?
Are you testing a twisted technique
of reverse waterboarding
in which you extract me from the womb
and pat me dry into a raisin
and you'll turn me into beef jerky
if I do not confess what I know
about the sex life of a ratted king?
Divorced, beheaded, died,
divorced, beheaded, survived?
Is that right?

I just pray that my parents
do not call me Catherine or Anne
because I may not be aware of my corporeal state yet
but I kind of like my head on my shoulders.

Do not call me Jane either.
No one remembers that one.
Is that what happens, Britain?
Is this how everyone does it?
Or have I been scammed?

15

SOFT POWER

Held in her mittens, mesmerised,
claws manicured in Union Jacks.
Copper and silver waters rise
inside a phone booth piggy bank.

Transmissions from the British Council,
where even the darkness seemed bright
across the ocean and the mountains.

Its radiance would glare on dry rivers,
electro beats bounced on accordions.
I used to wear a Westwood spacesuit.
Oxygen imported from London,
Liverpool, Manchester, anywhere,
all the same in that island.

I had convinced myself
the specks of dust were glitter,
that crying in Received Pronunciation
trumped fricative belly laughs.

The mirage took over my big brown eyes,
clogged my ears, nose and heart,
hijacking vocal cords.

Following the illusion
sat me down on a rocket –
or was it the tail of a comet?

By the time I reached Britannia,
I realised the light
that had guided me here
had taken centuries to reach my system.

By the time I had Britannia
in my mittens and claws,
cactus, snake and eagle,
she became supernova:

the sudden reignition
of nuclear fusion
in a degenerate star.

ACENTO

I take this *lengua madre*
a todas partes, como un perro
que persigue al sol.

Llevo esta mother tongue
anywhere, just like a dog
chasing the sun.

Cuando hablo y notan
que no soy de aquí,
preguntan: where's that accent from?

Respondo: Mexico.
Ah, Mehikoh!
I went there for a stag do.

Where to?
Can't remember.
I was very drunk.

Sin embargo,
yo recuerdo cómo y dónde estuve
cuando vine al Reino Unido.

Tuve que estar en mis cinco sentidos
pa' que no me deportaran
como persona non grata.

In spite of my sober arrival
I was well aware it could be over
any time I spoke.

Tracing my footprints in the snow,
no flakes, but eggshells.
Soft power turning hard around the edges.

Yet, *mi lengua madre* is a pillow
on which I can rest my feet
while I cherish origin and destination.

By the way,
my accent is from here.
The journey is still my home.

ROLE MODEL CITIZEN

What about those hearts war-torn,
too obfuscated to learn our new tongue,
broken ankles, no thumbs,
whose version of climbing Kilimanjaro is to go to the shops?

I am tired of success stories and smoothly adapted migrants –
but not too smoothly, please.
Keep the funny accent and still mean it when you sing 'God
Save the Queen',
but do not listen to anything not ethnic.
Do not watch EastEnders. Do not threaten
to take my job and do not make anything more
than friends with my daughters and sons –
no more than memories too blank for shellshock.

Thank you for these scraps.
For accepting my kidney money for a maroon passport
I soon must change to blue.

What about those migrant birds with suitcases on their spines?
Perpetual aching necks, too many pillows.
No actors, no spokespeople, no models for Calvin Klein.

I am too scared to apply for benefits
months after being naturalised
because the fear still creeps
that the postman will not deliver
my rejection letter for Universal Credit
because Home Office kicked down my door
to drag me into the van on the way to Yarl's Wood.

How would a postman slip a letter through a door
if there is no door?

Major drain on the NHS. Artery clog on the libraries.
What about those with the missing limbs

and the missing disk space for new memories?
'Cause not everyone is here to be a hero;
some are just here to subsist.

There are no rewards to go get groceries.
No ceremonial pomp to go toilet to piss.
No imperial march to chuck a monkey on the leccy on a very
good week.
Climbing the Swiss Alps is walking past your front room.
Climbing the Swiss Alps is having a front room to walk past.
Either way, what would we do with a medal
if we do not even know what to do with the shadows we cast?

CONFISCATED ROSARIES

Your pilgrimage across the rivers and the deserts halts on ice;
here come its agents.
They confiscate your rosaries
'cause there's no room for faith in purgatory.
White Jesus told them to detain you
and trap your songbirds in their cages.
God Emperor sits to the right;
the world's fate throbs under his thumbs.
His contacts above won't hear you,
bullet earplugs blasting reruns of Fox News.

So there's no point, they say, in you
wearing discontinued devices
around your swollen wrists
to communicate with saints of alabaster.
The apostles hide in the office kitchen,
washing down copper supplements with Diet Coke.
No way they will pick up the phone.
Plus you're the baddies, say the scriptures:
the gospel according to Alex Jones.
Deep in your heart, you know this will be temporary,

but time expands and shrinks
according to law enforcement whims –
every second you're locked in
is one second too many.
Your fingers will work as beads for now.
You count each Ave María;
your virgin apparition
resembles your ancestors
more than your captors:
complexion of soil and sand.

wearing flowers on her womb.
Four petals – cardinal arrows
that will guide you to your destination.
Your mother wraps the sky across your shoulders

and she whispers:
Piltsintli,
aquí no termina el viaje.
Beloved child,
the journey is not over yet.
We will get you out of this.

getting it along that I'm doing right now
... is not art is not
... thing that I'm doing right
... is not art is not art [also
        Found die on the dashboard
... the fall ... is not art
... is not art and ... the picture is that ...
        What I'm doing right now
        is a ... art is no longer
... that ... thing doing right
... are not ... doing ... it ...
                as it's ...
... that I'm doing ...
... not ... to the ...
his thing ... that I'm doing
... right now ... is not ...

THE SUCCESSFUL QUEER

BUT IS IT ART?

Falling is an art,
and what I'm doing right now is mass media.

It is kitsch,
foam die on a dartboard,
fall, die as I hear your name
and remember your picture.

What I'm doing right now is a bastard,
a spawn, mum at the waiting room of the clinic,
burst out from her abdomen as it's summoned for termination.
Determination.

This thing that I'm doing right now
is as stubborn and loud
as a white cis male, middle-class and middle-aged,
pitching the plot for the next comedy film
starring Adam Sandler.

This
is intimidating.
It speaks up, muffles any original thought
and rubs my right leg as it smirks and implores me
to give him a smile.

This…
falling…
is a telenovela villain
rolling down the stairs,
meeting her comeuppance.
As the stuntman touches the ground
and the first actress takes up his place,
she holds her breath to pretend she's dead,
but, eyes closed,
we can see she's still blinking.

Falling is an art,
yet I'm an imposter.
This thing I'm doing right now
is not art.

EFFECTIVE RECYCLING

The corpse in the garden looks at me,
although her eyes were devoured
long ago by the hornets next door.
She is too big for the compost bin,
yet I believe she could be a great fertiliser.

Animals, minerals and plants
are made of the same main components.
It would not be too farfetched
to grow daffodils out of her kidneys,
to feed roses with her heart,
to hydroponically grow basil in her lungs.
Only a few chromosomes make the difference
between humans and lettuce.

If we pulverised the bones,
scattered them over the jasmine bushes,
slugs could not suckle the flowers dry.
So I will chop her to pieces with a butter knife
and donate her to the Salvation Army;
they will know what to do with a sinner.

THE GIRL ELECTRIC

Electrocution
in small amounts
can galvanise,
reanimate.

If you want a dormant woman,
look at the mountains,
read fairy tales;
this one's wide awake.

When jungles
are burial sites
or awkwardly
constructed dams,
charring dead trees from their roots
can reforest –

not always,
of course.
But right now,
this girl blooms.

Right now,
this girl glows.
She always did,
but she did not know she could.

A fading lamp,
batteries running low,
fully solar charged –
she has always been the sun.

A glowing star,
a scorching being,
a celestial body
fuelled by laser beams

and her own sense of self
finally found,

step by step,
zap by zap,
hunch to jump,
murmur to shout.

Now she sings the girl electric
and the power is never out.

FEELING BACKWARD

Negatives, inverted memories.
Recollections doomed from the beginning.
Buried by the dead, quarantined by the living.

Social dissolution, gold leaf, deadnamed captions.
Seldom perpendicular performances.
Doric columns crumble in the white cube.

Celebrate or retrograde.
Psychic trains, forever late,
fall into the well of loneliness.

The museum of same love
often forgets
sodium sculptures,

inadequately stored
behind MDF walls
covered in rainbows.

Corroding EDM,
on blast to drown their wails.
Everybody's free but the unlovable.
The art of losing is not for a refined taste.

The angel of history has been denied the chance to meet us.

RECOGNISE

for Khadija Saye

Recognise women and nonbinary artists while they are around.
Recognise women and nonbinary artists of colour while they
    are around.
Recognise working-class women and nonbinary artists of colour
    while they are around.
Recognise queer working-class women and nonbinary artists of
    colour while they are around.
 Recognise queer working-class women and nonbinary artists of
    colour who don't fulfil mainstream thincentric Western
    beauty standards while they are around.
Recognise them before they burn out. Before you burn them
    out. Don't burn them out.
Recognise them before they fade away. Don't let them fade
    away.

THE CHILD PRODIGY

ESCALA DE INTELIGENCIA
VERBAL   P.B.   P.E.
7
3   7
10
8   9
5   8
4
6   13
10   14
drive,
on the
urso
till
ne.
relatively
lower at
ADHD
thia wri
y takin
her
hard to
ng she
learned
her tablet
ext on a
ould be
n her
se she
has
that
efers to
hold op
ding as the lin
year old Toshiba
2GHz AMD A8
rk checker. This
software and will
old for USA soft
combined p
previously u

BECOMING

Back then, I was my grandma's couch,
watching telenovelas
after game shows and the news.
Back then, I was my granddad's bachelor tall bed.
I was, simultaneously,
the princess and the pea.

I was detergent bottle flowerpots.
I was gore and guns, spicy comedies,
the calendar of Laura León in 1992.
I was long baths on the washboard,
avocados raining on the rooftop.
I was dusty books on Spanish history
and thick magazines on royal families.

I became a perfume sample,
scratch and sniff right off the page.
Ocean Dream,
a crown of mountains,
drowned in five large cups of coffee a day
and first infatuations.
I became a Discman,
the skips on a burnt CD-R
and over a hundred MP3s on shopping road trips.

I became sinister.
Still tasted like a baby.
Suppressed memories,
sleepovers,
120 Minutes.

I became 1998,
I became 2001,
I became the World Trade Center and King's Cross St Pancras.

I no longer was what I should have been
and the bed got smaller.
No flowers,
no detergent bottle flowerpots,
no magazines.

LITTLE GIRL

You are not a girl,
you are not little,
yet your body
is not big enough
to contain you.

That bow on your head,
those shoes and dress
are as effective to retrain you
as they are to anchor you
to the therapist's chair
at the audio-phoniatric centre.

They certainly do not deter you
from running outside and jumping
into the outdoors swimming pool.

October,
frilly socks and petticoat,
damp dog.

DIAGNOSTIC STUDIES: 1990-2018

Generally joyful, extroverted,
disobeying orders.
Only stopped by sudden noises.
Caring, loving. Fear of darkness.
Never naps.
Acceptable gross motor skills,
fine motor skills not fine.
Operative receptive language,
reality incongruently managed.
Discreetly diminished linguistic aspects.
Unrepressed curiosity and continuous locution.
Intolerance towards frustration,
no visual contact in communication.
Dexterity, semiotics, problem solving,
rich distraction, poor attention,
difficult oral expression, environment adaptation.
High execution, low speech, three months younger in maturity.
Indulgence, firmness and stimuli:
keys to task achievement.
Nothing that therapy and school cannot control.

Reading accuracy high,
speed slightly lower.
Difficult reading materials,
taking notes if there is no interest.
Thoughts taking over.
Distraction-prone, clumsy,
like all those years ago.
Hard to motivate oneself
when overwhelmed by all to-dos.
Symptoms of visual stress.
Light text on dark background works best.
Text-to-speech, podcasts, speedread twice
or more to absorb.
Hard to determine salient points:
underline, highlight, annotations.

Overachiever,
two master's degrees,
somehow too few.
Mentorship and technology will do.
Nothing that therapy and school still cannot solve.

MALL DEL NORTE

Destiny manifested itself
at the changing rooms of the JCPenney
contained within Laredo's Mall del Norte.

Like every teenager, I was unbearable:
diets, hair dye, braces, a quinceañera,
fruitless procedures to make friends at school.

I thought it would be super cool
if I practised my English
during one of our Texas shopping trips.

I asked the clerk,
Can I get this in red?
She said,
Claro, m'ijita. Deja te lo traigo.

Half-naked and ashamed, I overheard
the clerk chat to her colleague in a mix
of southern English and northern Spanish.

I remembered that this land used to be ours.
That over 200 years after being sold,
fingers crossed on our backs,
to the United States of America,
only a violent river and a more violent bureaucracy
kept us apart from each other.

Some of our people were included in the trade.
We did not cross the border,
said Eva Longoria.
The border crossed us.

Even those who did cross,
like a third of my extended family,
nurtured this state so deeply,
bare hands sculpting each household
like mountains, part of the earth.

When the clerk came back
with a size 14 red top from the juniors' section,
I mumbled *gracias* as my hand reached out.

She said,
You welcome, m'ijita. Aquí estoy if you need anything.
Here I am. Here we are.

MY KIND

My kind are everywhere, and so am I.
My kind are bubbles floating, spreading, bursting and being
    blown again.
My kind are confused by time zones, but they can still easily
    navigate them.
My kind have translators in one hand and dictionaries in
    the other. One to explain themselves to others and one to
    understand the world. None of them work, but my kind use
    them anyway.
If you hold my kind's bags, you may ask yourself, *What are
    they carrying? Rocks?* The answer is yes.
My kind carry the founding stones of their identity wherever
    they go, pick up new pebbles along the way and add them to
    their collection.
My kind might feel awkward in public, so they wear makeup as
    war paint and clothing as chainmail.
My kind delete chain mail as soon as they read the title.
My kind are not superstitious, but they tell you to be quiet
    when Walter Mercado speaks the fate of their stars.
My kind are clumsy tarmac mermaids, stumbling everywhere,
    still trying to get used to their legs.
My kind were called names in school. Now they have adopted
    these names as their own. Names used for reconstruction
    instead of destruction.
My kind think twice about their adverbs.
My kind struggled trying to write the word 'adverbs', but they
    eventually did it, and that is a triumph.
My kind, I repeat, are everywhere.
And so am I. Do not mess with us.

THE PERFECT BODY

LIVE MODEL

My image is yours for a moment.
Keep staring and get the proportions
as right or as wrong as you imagine.
The volume, the charcoal,

the lights and the darkness,
your fingers get darker,
the paper gets thinner
in contact with matter.

I sit on the mattress,
slight twist of the spine.
I stare at the ceiling,
imagine the sky.

Cracks, peels and fingerprints,
like someone has tried
to paint an eclipse.
Another live model, perhaps.

Right now,
my image is yours,
but forever
the heavens are mine.

TEXTILE WORKSHOP

Make it out of blouses you never wear as they make you look square,
cobwebs peeping out from the space between buttons bursting from
    your breasts.

Make it out of modesty used as a death sentence.
Tear those flowery tops to shreds before the sleeves cut off all
    circulation.

Make it out of trousers forcibly acquired with your mother's money,
swearing they were essentials when they were essentially not there.
Pocket effect to fool you into trying to hide your hands,
nothing but flappy rectangles on random parts of your thighs.
Rip them up and sew a cocoon to rest.

Make it out, for goodness' sake, of all your professional workwear,
the clothes you wear to interviews to disguise your authenticity,
only to find you were too bland to succeed.

Make it out of your big clothes, small clothes, passive-aggressive
    presents,
the hues of the ground where you are meant to be buried,
not of the sky where you are destined to fly.

Make it out of mum jeans larger than your mum.
Make it out of dad flannels dustier than your dad.
Make it out of the solitary rack at the end of the retail store,
the novelty act at the fashion show,
the cold pat on the shoulder at the primetime beauty advert.
Break it, smear it, shred it, shame it, trash into magnificence.
Paint it with more colours than the human eye can see.

THE SIZE OF A PENCIL

You still remember your last supper,
before you died on the surgery plank
and resurrected several months later.

The size of a pencil.
The oven is the size of a pencil.
More guests come to dine,
but the oven is the size of a pencil.

You sliced, diced and eradicated
the concept of me,
the concept of you
and the concept of them
from the head of the table.

You could have stayed me
had you not signed the contract,
had you not paid the deposit
for a downsized bungalow.

You are offended I am grey work
across the road from your masterpiece.
That I remind you of your wirings, pipelines,
bricks, nails and foam.

My impending demolition is not a reason to cry,
but to you the real treason
is that my sprinklers squeak
that the grass is greener on your side.

That, you see, is the real problem,
and not that for me to succeed
I must move from A to B
and that is an insult to C.

You are hungry, you are angry, and you are shouting
paragraphs against my columns.

You feel betrayed because I wish I could join,
receive VIP passes on the post
and visit gardens that right now I do not know –
and I probably never will –

because I am built like a shithouse.

My oven is a toilet.
Your oven is the size of a pencil,
and a pencil is all you need
to write.

SUMMER BODY/CHRISTMAS CORPSE

This summer body
brings a Christmas corpse.
The war of attrition
is a red balloon.
Whenever I take it,
it swallows me whole;
when I try to ignore it,
it just never goes
away.

What happened to you?

I have lost everything by gaining.
I have lost everything
by trying to lose.
I have lost everything by gaining.
I have lost everything;
now I am losing you.

Summer body,
Christmas corpse.

All this volume
made of void.
Not a galaxy,
a black hole.

SPIDERGIRLS

There are girls who have one leg.

There are girls who have one leg.
There are girls who have two legs.
There are girls who have three legs.

There are girls who have three legs but wish they had just two.
There are girls who have one leg who wish they had one more.
There are girls who have two legs and wish that they had
none.

Regardless of legs,
there are girls who are not mums
and there are boys who are mums.

Regardless of legs,
there are girls who love boys who will not touch them at all.
Girls who love girls who will fondle them all.
Both or neither, who love both or neither, and get both or
neither.

Regardless of legs,
there are girls whose boys, girls, neither, both,
have abandoned them because
the torso they carry on their legs is too much.
The head they carry on their shoulders is too much.
The skin is a very heavy coat they are not willing to carry.

The legs are too many.
The legs are too few.
So they set them alight and depart.

Sometimes they never come around.
Or they confuse you and come back in the dark,
where documentary filmmakers cannot roll their cameras and
ask

if they still love them and why.
There are girls, boys, neither, both,
who stare at empty cots and baby shoes,
or who sprawl across their living rooms.

Their lives are not international
and their bodies are never loved.
Either way, they do not aim for love,
but for good old survival.

Because it is hard to embrace yourself when your wrists are
handcuffed.
It is hard to embrace yourself when your hands are tied.
It is hard to embrace yourself when your arms are short.

And when, regardless of the number of your legs,
civilisation treats you like you have more than eight,
the best thing you can do is climb and build your own web.

idence to know that you do not have
or an exemption or
a prescrip-
to provide ev
levant bene
HAPPY INSIDE
ur prescriptio... ...s fre
ement later if you do not sh
ou have to pay a prescripti
art 2 the amount
u cannot show evidence
e but NHS Englan
't award notice
Evidence. You may
to pay. You could show t
pre-payment certificate.
iter
t that time you can stil
ay arrange to check you
h about Penalty Charges

THE BEAUTIFUL MIND

HOW TO LEAVE THE HOUSE IN TIMES OF TROUBLE

First, open your eyes.
If you do not open your eyes, you will not know what you are missing
and you will not know what to call out if possible.
Have any medication you require:
water, antidepressants, herbal remedies, a wank.

Get up and, if you can, have a shower.
If you feel Herculean enough, have breakfast and a shower
or shower and a breakfast.
Superheroes prefer an English full Monty
or, to stay in touch, a continental.
For basic self-preservation, make a smoothie or chug a yoghurt.
You need the fruits to bring back colour to your skin.

Get dressed. Wear something pretty and revealing,
but not revealing enough to attract negative attention.
You want a dress to hug your curves, not hands to suffocate them.
When you feel stronger and ready to fight back, run naked down
    the road
wearing nothing but a Swiss knife hanging from a necklace.

Put on your makeup.
You may cry while putting on eyeliner.
If that happens, put it on again.
Have makeup remover within your arm's reach,
and your phone next to it to call 999.
Can you text 999 instead?
Tweet 999 if possible.

Wear comfy shoes.
Do not be scared of betraying your gender or lack thereof.
You are still a woman in trainers.
You are still a man in stilettos.

You are still a person in boots.
I recommend boots,
in case you piss yourself and want to avoid soaking your socks
    in the puddles.
Or, much better, in case your enemies piss themselves,
terrified by the fact
that you are not afraid to leave the house –
even if you are, nobody needs to know.

Now get your umbrella,
get your sunglasses,
get your keys
and open the door.

…FOR YESTERDAY

Lying dead on the lines,
belly-down, as if praying
for an extension.

Around me, workers race
through the book of hours.
Calloused feet, friction matches
against vellum and parchment.

Lapis lazuli in flames,
gold and silver details –
no time for dear illustrations.

I want it for yesterday,
belts the volcano through his furnaced face.

Blood for exposure,
sweat for experience,
read my ideas like you live on my mind.

They feed buckets
of net sacrifice
right into his mouth,
virgins and elders alike.

Limbs wrapped in jewellery
like tinfoil engulfing a spud.
Dressed to the nines
until five and beyond.

The volcano drank all clocks for breakfast.
The day only ends when he burps
every alarm from the depths
of the spring in his belly.

I tried to run,
but my ankles defeated me.
I tossed my bucket in panic
before hitting the ground –

all products of my labour
absorbed by the soil.
Wrists and chest took the impact,
expelled all breath from my lungs.

When I woke up from the shock,
everyone else had gone home.
This job was for yesterday,
and now I pray for deferral.

I WANT TO BELIEVE IN MYSELF AS MUCH AS I BELIEVE IN MY PLANTS

My housemate said, *Word of advice:*
this is the place where plants come to die.

I took the warning as a challenge.
Now they are on my list of plans.
I have become hyperfixated
on doing my best to see them thrive.

I give them water, soil and sunshine.
By the front window is where they lie.
I ask my pals, proper green fingers,
for tips on keeping them alive.

Could the near-flatlines catch new rhythms?
I give brown twigs a second chance.

All they need is someone who believes
and speaks to them not expecting back
phrases, but maybe a few new sprouts.
Who knows? Might be their time to rise.

Is it my time to rise, I wonder?
I might need to weed out all doubts.
I need some water, soil and sunshine.
Lie by the window, have a chat.

Contrary to mainstream belief
I am as well a living being.
I need somebody to believe
and dedicate their space and time.

That somebody needs to be me,

because while words and acts of love

are sent my way, the blinds are down,
the windows shut, my soil is dry,
no tears can slip in through the cracks.
The shit I feel could be manure
if I process it well enough.

I know that phrase about loving yourself
before loving anybody else
is a simplistic ableist myth,

but if I cannot love myself for now
I can believe, or make believe,
as much as I believe in my plants.

PEPPER SPRAY

Yet I am here, yet I still came,
but if you touch me, pepper spray.
Can you believe the tables turned
in such a devastating way?

You stand and shake, pretend you bend,
prepare yourself another face.
If in the centre you are not placed,
the world will crumble in your name.

Your voice is loud and interrupts
all people's actions, words and thoughts.
The universe your nursery.
Your wounded manhood, monolith.

With heavy boots, your weak feet stomp
on ants, and then complain it hurts.
Caveats are there for you to break,
then put the blame on those who care.

What if I told you that your moves
and your erratic protocols
sent this one straight into the hole?
Into the point of no return?

All broken bones and broken dreams,
rushing oneself to A&E.
Tears through the hallways, all confused.
I could not find the self I lost.

An afternoon of screeching teeth,
an urgency to peel the skin
like a cucumber beauty mask,
but leaving flesh and nerves behind.

You only think about yourself;
you only fight for your own rights.
Now every time I see your face,
rush into a state of flight or fight.

There is nowhere to hide away,
there is no place we can call home:
all sanctuaries now desecrated,
walls smeared with blood on every school.

Want to contain the need to scream
and dig a hole under the sea.
Yet I am here, yet I still came,
but if you touch me, pepper spray.

BRITNEY NEW VEGAS

She rises from nuclear apocalypse.
Locks of hair salted in ashes
of souvenirs from Planet Hollywood.
Survived 2007, 2017,
'19 and '20, barely.

She had survived underage titillation,
skimpy uniform,
chewing gum, exploitation.
Forced to beg for desire, puppy eyes,
yet pretend purity.
Until that one bad boyfriend,
childhood friend, musketeer,
stole the cheese, unfolding a chain of events
represented on *Buffy*
as a journey through a factory in hell.

The surrounding debris
a mirror through her soul,
early aughts.
That is the chapel
where Jason and I got married,

she is reminded by a lone standing column
wrapped in ivy.
What is it with me and childhood buddies?
Adult bodies, keeping hold of their memories
as radiation seeps in.

Her two children at the Institute:
quantum scientists in their seventies,
exploring the links between AI and resilience.
The blood sample for their bots
came from their mum.

She has gone through blasts, blackouts,
terrible friendships, cultists, managers,

war, famine, pestilence and death.
Just like her, the planet has changed,
although she has not changed on the outside.

Once she reaches the border
between Nevada and Louisiana,
Britney raises her sight
into the eternal sunset:
It's been so darn long since I've painted the sky.

MEANWHILE

Jumping into the shadows,
jumping out of the shadows,
on and off, through our liminal journeys.

Doors forever revolving,
letting in, kicking out
the people and places we were, and we are.

We might seem a bit scared;
that is what we will say,
but secretly we cannot wait for what is next.

For the next big jump,
back into the Meanwhile,
because that is where we are going to find it.

That is where I will find you.
That is where you will find me.
We will find the meaning. We will find the meaning.

GLOSSARY, NOTES AND CREDITS

Liminal Inhabitant
Liminality: a concept defined by Arnold van Gennep and
    developed by Victor Turner. The threshold in the middle of
    a rite of passage, in which a person is no longer who they
    were before the rite while not yet having reached the form or
    status they are meant to achieve once the rite is completed.

Naturalisation
Based on the experience of taking the Life in the UK test, the
theory exam required for migrants in the United Kingdom to
achieve settlement and/or citizenship status. Often criticised for
being history-focused rather than dealing more with necessary
information for daily life.

Soft Power
Soft power: a political term introduced by Joseph S Nye Jr
    which refers to the non-coercive ways in which a country co-
    opts talent and capital by using attractive elements such as
    culture, policies and values.

Acento
The first two stanzas translate each other. The rest of the Spanish
sections mean:

> *Cuando hablo y notan*
> *que no soy de aqui,*
> *preguntan:*

'When I speak and they notice that I am not from here, they
ask:'

> *Respondo:*

'I answer:'

> *Sin embargo,*
> *yo recuerdo cómo y dónde estuve*
> *cuando vine al Reino Unido.*

'Nevertheless, I remember how and where I was when I came to the United Kingdom.'

> *Tuve que estar en mis cinco sentidos*
> *pa' que no me deportaran*
> *como persona non grata.*

'I had to be in my five senses so I would not get deported as persona non grata.'

Role Model Citizen
EastEnders: thirty-plus-year-old soap opera from the BBC.
   Takes place in the fictional community of Walford, in the East
   End of London.
Universal Credit: social security payment for low-income or
   unemployed British citizens.
Home Office: governmental department in charge of migration.
Yarl's Wood: Yarl's Wood Immigration Removal Centre, a
   detention camp in which 'illegal immigrants' are held
   indefinitely before deportation. One of the largest facilities
   of its kind in Europe. Mostly holds women and children.
NHS: National Health Service, British healthcare system funded
by taxpayers.
Chuck a monkey on the leccy: top up the electricity meter with
   £20 worth of electricity.

Confiscated Rosaries
Based on a photograph taken by Tom Kiefer, former janitor at a US Customs and Border Patrol facility in Arizona, featuring several rosaries which were seized from detainees and discarded by officers. Kiefer had rescued these personal faith objects from the bin.

The virgin apparition in question is the Virgen de Guadalupe, Mexico's manifestation of Virgin Mary.

The four next-to-last lines translate each other from Náhuatl and Spanish into English.

But Is It Art?
Adam Sandler: North American actor, famous for starring in blockbuster comedies and art films.
Telenovela: the Latin American version of soap operas. Shorter in lifespan, more intense in content.

Effective Recycling
An earlier version of this poem was published in *Queer Zine* (ed. Dean Atta, Mouthy Poets, 2016).

Feeling Backward
Inspired by the book *Feeling Backward: Loss and the Politics of Queer History* by Heather Love.

Recognise
This poem was used in the song of the same name by the band Anatomy, album *You're Nothing to Me* (Circle House Records, 2018).

Khadija Saye: Gambian-British photographer and care worker whose work was exhibited at the Venice Biennale shortly before her death in the Grenfell Tower fire of 2017.

Becoming
Laura León: Mexican singer and telenovela star, protagonist of Dos Mujeres Un Camino, featuring Mexican-American actor Erik Estrada.
Ocean Dream: perfume by Giorgio Beverly Hills.
120 Minutes: alternative/indie music programme from MTV.

Little Girl
An earlier version of this poem will be used in the upcoming album by Coventry band Nim Chimpsky.
Audio-phoniatric centre: therapy centre focused on audiology, speech, physical and mental development.

Mall Del Norte
JCPenney: USA department store.
Eva Longoria: USA actress of Mexican heritage.
Quinceañera: a lavish Mexican party often preceded by a

Catholic mass, taking place on a teenage girl's fifteenth birthday to celebrate her passage from childhood into 'womanhood'.

Claro, m'ijita. Deja te lo traigo: 'of course, my little daughter. Let me bring it to you.
Gracias: 'Thank you.'
Aquí estoy: 'Here I am.'

My Kind
Walter Mercado: extravagant Puerto Rican astrologer who provided horoscopes on Latin-American media for almost fifty years.

Live Model
An earlier version of this poem was featured in *The Time Travellers Write* (self-published zine, 2017).

Textile Workshop
An earlier version of this poem was performed live by the artist in collaboration with musician David Dhonau at the multidisciplinary event The Image Is the Servant (De Montfort University, 2017).

Summer Body/Christmas Corpse
This poem was used in the song of the same name by the musical project Birthgiver (2018).

Spidergirls
An earlier version of this poem was published in the Black Flamingo Zine (eds Dean Atta and Ben Connors, Tate Britain, 2017).

How to Leave the House in Times of Trouble
An earlier version of this poem was published in *Your Feelings Are Valid: Fan Club Zine #11* (Fan Club Notts, 2017).

Britney New Vegas
What if USA performer Britney Spears were a character in Bethesda videogame Fallout: New Vegas?

Buffy: short for Buffy the Vampire Slayer, television series about a teenage girl who hunts vampires and other supernatural villains. The episode referenced is 'Anne', series 3 episode 1.

ACKNOWLEDGEMENTS

First and foremost, I want to thank the Leicester spoken word scene – especially nights such as Find the Right Words, WORD! and Anerki – for granting me space for expression these past five years, inspiring me to go further and showing me some of the ways poetry could be paired and performed on stage.

Thank you also to Mouthy Poets in Nottingham – particularly Anne Holloway, Debris Stevenson, Dean Atta and Chris McLoughlin – for embracing me when I was young in age and career. Although we officially met each other for a relatively short time, those months were formative and have lightened my path ever since.

Infinite gratitude for Bridget Hart, Clive Birnie and Shagufta Iqbal from Burning Eye Books for believing in me at a stage at which I did not believe in myself. Thanks to Jess Green for your mentoring and for being a treasure locally and worldwide.

Finally, I want to thank family, friends and loved ones for being there and staying there. None of this would have been possible without you.